Gooseberry Patch®

Our Favorite Chocolate Recipes

Copyright 2005, Gooseberry Patch
First Printing, December, 2005

Types of chocolate and their uses

Milk chocolate:
> Pure chocolate mixed with extra cocoa butter and
> sugar. Sweet, smooth and a favorite for snackers.

Dark chocolate:
> Pure chocolate with a smooth, rich flavor; not quite as sweet as milk
> chocolate. Use either dark or milk chocolate in candy-making and baking,
> depending on your personal preference.

Semi-sweet chocolate:

> Pure chocolate perfection. Available in chunks or chips,
> semi-sweet chocolate has less sugar content and is just
> right for making chocolate chip cookies or muffins.

Melting chocolate:

Perfect for dipping strawberries and making your own homemade candies. For a real chocolate fix (or quick, thoughtful gift) dip double-cream chocolate sandwich cookies (store-bought) into melted milk or dark chocolate. Let set, then drizzle with melted white chocolate.

Baking cocoa:

Use for baking cakes, brownies, making frostings and hot chocolate. Extra bonus: baking cocoa is naturally low in fat and cholesterol-free. A good low-fat

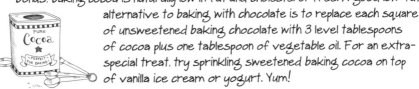

alternative to baking with chocolate is to replace each square of unsweetened baking chocolate with 3 level tablespoons of cocoa plus one tablespoon of vegetable oil. For an extra-special treat, try sprinkling sweetened baking cocoa on top of vanilla ice cream or yogurt. Yum!

Having a mug of chocolatey cocoa? Make it irresistible by adding
a favorite hard candy and stirring until melted. Try orange,
peppermint or raspberry...great for coffee, too!

Double Chocolate Chip Muffins

Makes 2 dozen

18-1/4 oz. pkg. chocolate fudge
    cake mix
3.9-oz. pkg. instant chocolate
    pudding mix
3/4 c. water
4 eggs, beaten

1/2 c. oil
1/2 t. almond extract
6-oz. pkg. mini semi-sweet
    chocolate chips, frozen
Garnish: powdered sugar

Blend cake mix, pudding mix, water, eggs, oil and extract until smooth; fold in chocolate chips. Fill muffin cups three-quarters full; bake at 350 degrees for 25 to 35 minutes. Cool; sprinkle with powdered sugar before serving.

The proof of the pudding is in the eating.

−Miguel de Cervantes

Hot Chocolate Muffins

Makes 1-1/2 to 2 dozen

1/2 c. butter, softened
1 c. sugar
4 eggs, separated
6 T. hot chocolate mix
1/2 c. boiling water

2/3 c. milk
3 c. all-purpose flour
2 T. baking powder
1 t. salt
2 t. vanilla extract

Blend butter and sugar together in a large mixing bowl until creamy; add egg yolks and beat until well blended. In a separate bowl, dissolve hot chocolate mix in boiling water; add to butter mixture with milk. Sift together flour, baking powder and salt; add to chocolate mixture. Beat egg whites and vanilla until stiff peaks form; fold into chocolate mixture. Pour batter into greased muffin cups. Bake at 375 degrees for 20 to 25 minutes, or until centers test done.

Short on time but need a dessert fast? Dip plump strawberries
or mandarin orange slices into melted semi-sweet chocolate.
Set on wax paper and chill until chocolate is firm.

Chocolate Chip Pancakes

Makes 12 to 16 pancakes

1 c. milk
2 eggs, beaten
2 c. buttermilk biscuit baking
    mix

1/4 t. cinnamon
1/2 c. mini semi-sweet
    chocolate chips
Optional: powdered sugar

Combine first 4 ingredients, stirring until moistened. Fold in chocolate chips, being sure not to overblend. Drop by 1/4 cupfuls onto a hot, greased griddle; flip over when bubbles appear around edges. Cook on each side until lightly golden. Sprinkle with powdered sugar, if desired.

For an extra-special treat, pour melted chocolate onto wax paper-lined cookie sheets and spread to 1/8-inch thickness. Refrigerate until firm and then cut shapes with mini cookie cutters. Remove from wax paper and chill. Garnish cakes, pies, even Chocolate Chip Waffles!

Chocolate Chip Waffles

Makes 6 servings

1-3/4 c. all-purpose flour
2 t. baking powder
1/2 t. salt
1-1/2 c. milk
1 T. butter, melted

1-1/2 t. vanilla extract
1 egg, separated
1 T. sugar
1/2 c. mini semi-sweet
    chocolate chips

Combine the first 3 ingredients in a large mixing bowl; set aside. Whisk milk, butter, vanilla and egg yolk together until frothy; add to flour mixture, stirring well. Set aside. Beat egg white until stiff peaks form; fold into flour mixture. Gently stir in chocolate chips. Pour by 1/2 cupfuls onto a hot, greased waffle iron; heat according to manufacturer's instructions.

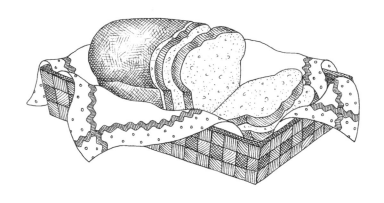

For even richer tasting hot cocoa, make it with chocolate milk!

Banana-Chocolate Chip Bread

Makes 2 loaves

3/4 c. butter, softened
1-1/2 c. sugar
3 eggs
3 bananas, mashed
3 c. all-purpose flour
1-1/2 t. baking soda

10-oz. jar maraschino cherries,
drained and 1/4 c. juice
reserved
6-oz. pkg. semi-sweet
chocolate chips

Mix all ingredients together in a large bowl. Pour into 2 greased
9"x5" loaf pans. Bake at 350 degrees for one hour.

Chocolate and raspberry are a heavenly combination! Try a dollop of raspberry jam sandwiched between 2 chocolatey cookies or warm raspberry jam spread on fresh-baked chocolate chip muffins for a no-fuss glaze.

Mocha Chip Muffins

Makes one to 1-1/2 dozen

1-oz. sq. unsweetened baking
  chocolate
1/2 c. margarine
1 c. milk
1 egg, beaten
1 t. vanilla extract
2 c. all-purpose flour

3/4 c. sugar
2-1/2 t. baking powder
2 t. instant coffee granules
1/2 t. salt
1/2 c. mini semi-sweet
  chocolate chips
1/4 c. black walnuts, chopped

In a small saucepan over low heat, melt chocolate square and
margarine together. Cool slightly. Whisk in milk, then egg and vanilla.
In a large mixing bowl, combine flour, sugar, baking powder, instant
coffee and salt. Stir in chocolate mixture until just blended. Mix in
mini chocolate chips and black walnuts. Spoon into greased muffin
cups. Bake at 375 degrees for 15 to 20 minutes.

A delicious treat anyone will enjoy! Melt a bag of semi-sweet chocolate chips...dip pretzels, raisins, crackers, marshmallows, peanut brittle, pecans, dried fruit or espresso beans. Pack into gift tins for giving.

Cappuccino Cooler

Makes 4 servings

1-1/2 c. prepared coffee, cooled
1-1/2 c. chocolate ice cream,
   softened
1/4 c. chocolate syrup

crushed ice
1 c. frozen whipped topping,
   thawed

Blend coffee, ice cream and syrup together until smooth; set aside.
Fill 4 glasses three-quarters full with ice; add coffee mixture. Top with
a spoonful of whipped topping; serve immediately. Makes 4 servings.

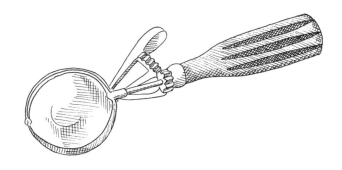

Coffee adds a rich taste to chocolate recipes… just substitute an equal amount for water or milk in cake, cookie or brownie recipes.

Chilly Chocolate Malts

Makes 2 servings

1 c. milk
1/2 c. caramel ice cream topping
2 c. chocolate ice cream,
   softened

3-1/2 T. malted milk powder
2 T. chopped pecans
Garnish: grated chocolate

Combine first 5 ingredients in a blender; cover and blend until smooth.
Pour into chilled glasses; sprinkle with grated chocolate.

Offer different types of chocolate as coffee
toppings...bittersweet, semi-sweet, milk and white chocolate.
Set out a bowl of lemon zest, whole cardamom pods, whipped
cream and a shaker of sugar to try too.

Chocolate Coffee Mix

Makes 2-3/4 cups mix

1/2 c. instant coffee granules
1-1/2 c. powdered non-dairy
    creamer
1/2 c. chocolate drink mix

1/4 c. sugar
1/8 t. salt
1/2 t. nutmeg

Mix all ingredients together in a blender. Add by teaspoonfuls to taste to a cup of hot water.

Teach us delight in simple things.
-Rudyard Kipling

Cinnamon Hot Chocolate

Makes 4 servings

1/4 c. baking cocoa
1/4 c. sugar
1 c. boiling water

3 c. milk
6-inch cinnamon stick
1 t. vanilla extract

Combine cocoa and sugar in a double boiler; slowly stir in water.
Return to a boil; boil for 2 minutes. Add milk and cinnamon stick.
Heat for 10 minutes over low heat; remove cinnamon stick and add
vanilla. Stir quickly to froth milk.

Top off a chocolatey mug of cocoa with a big dollop of whipped cream. Set a mini cookie cutter on top and gently sprinkle baking cocoa inside...carefully remove the cutter to reveal the design.

Chocolate Chip Cheese Ball

Makes about 2 cups

8-oz. pkg. cream cheese,
   softened
1/2 c. butter, softened
1/4 t. vanilla extract
3/4 c. powdered sugar

2 T. brown sugar, packed
3/4 c. mini semi-sweet
   chocolate chips
3/4 c. chopped pecans
sugar cookies, vanilla wafers

Combine cream cheese, butter and vanilla; blend until fluffy. Add sugars; mix well. Fold in chocolate chips. Cover and refrigerate for 2 hours. Shape dough into a ball; cover with plastic wrap and refrigerate for one hour. Uncover and roll in pecans before serving. Serve with sugar cookies and vanilla wafers for dipping.

Top a warm, flaky waffle with vanilla ice cream, chocolate syrup and a dollop of whipped cream to create a tasty waffle sundae!

Chocolate Fruit Dip

Makes about 2 cups

8-oz. pkg. cream cheese,
  softened
1 c. powdered sugar
1/4 c. baking cocoa

1/4 c. milk
Optional: 1/4 t. orange extract
assorted fresh fruit for dipping

Beat cream cheese with an electric mixer on medium speed until
fluffy. Blend in powdered sugar, cocoa, milk and orange extract, if
using. Beat on medium speed until smooth. Cover and refrigerate
several hours or overnight for flavors to blend. Serve chilled with
sliced fruit for dipping.

Melt together 24 ounces semi-sweet chocolate chips,
6 tablespoons corn syrup and one pint whipping cream for
a chocolate fondue that's out of this world!

Caramel-Filled Chocolate Cookies

Makes 4 dozen

2-1/4 c. all-purpose flour
3/4 c. baking cocoa
1 t. baking soda
1 c. plus 1 T. sugar, divided
1 c. brown sugar, packed
1 c. margarine, softened

2 eggs, beaten
2 t. vanilla extract
1 c. chopped pecans, divided
48 chocolate-covered caramels,
    unwrapped

Combine flour, cocoa and baking soda; set aside. In a medium mixing bowl, combine one cup sugar, brown sugar and margarine until fluffy. Stir in eggs and vanilla. Slowly add flour mixture and 1/2 cup pecans; mix well and set aside. Combine remaining sugar and pecans in a separate bowl; set aside. For each cookie, shape one tablespoon of dough around one chocolate-covered caramel. Dip one side of each cookie into nut mixture; arrange on ungreased baking sheets, dipped-side up. Bake at 375 degrees for 7 to 10 minutes; cool on baking sheets for 2 minutes before removing to wire racks to cool completely.

Looking for a smooth velvety chocolate glaze for cookies, cakes or brownies? Melt together one cup chocolate chips with 3 tablespoons corn syrup, 2-1/4 teaspoons water and 1/4 cup shortening. Quick, easy and so good!

Chewy Chocolate Cookies

Makes 4-1/2 dozen

1-1/4 c. butter, softened
2 c. sugar
2 eggs, beaten
2 t. vanilla extract

2 c. all-purpose flour
3/4 c. baking cocoa
1 t. baking soda
1/2 t. salt

Blend butter and sugar until creamy; add eggs and vanilla. Mix well and set aside. Combine flour, cocoa, baking soda and salt; blend into butter mixture. Drop by teaspoonfuls onto ungreased baking sheets. Bake at 350 degrees for 8 to 9 minutes; do not overbake. Cookies will be soft and will flatten while cooling.

When shipping cookies, place pieces of wax paper between
cookie layers and add mini marshmallows to make sure
cookies don't move around. Tuck in a couple packages
of cocoa for a great gift.

Quick Chocolate Cookies

Makes 2 dozen

9-oz. pkg. devil's food cake mix
1 egg, beaten
1 T. shortening, melted

1/2 c. chopped nuts
2 T. water

Combine all ingredients; mix well. Drop by teaspoonfuls onto ungreased baking sheets. Bake at 350 degrees for 10 minutes; cool on wire racks.

A simple treat...dip banana slices into melted chocolate and then roll in mini chocolate chips. Place on a baking sheet and freeze to make a frosty snack.

Banana-Chocolate Chip Cookies

Makes 4 dozen

1/2 c. sugar
1 egg, beaten
1/3 c. shortening
1/2 c. banana, mashed
1 c. all-purpose flour
1/4 t. salt

1 t. baking powder
1/2 t. baking soda
1/2 t. vanilla extract
1 c. semi-sweet chocolate chips
Optional: 1/2 c. chopped nuts

Blend sugar, egg and shortening together; mix in banana. Add flour, salt, baking powder, baking soda and vanilla; mix well. Fold in chocolate chips and nuts, if desired. Drop by tablespoonfuls onto greased baking sheets; bake at 375 degrees for 12 to 15 minutes. Let cool 2 minutes on sheets before removing to wire racks to cool completely.

Make a chocoholic gift basket! Fill it with gourmet cocoa,
chocolate-dipped peppermint sticks and pretzels, chewy brownies,
chocolate-peanut butter fudge, double chocolate cookies and
cocoa-dusted truffles...a chocolate lover's dream!

BIG Chocolate Cookies

Makes 6 dozen

2 18-1/4 oz. pkgs. chocolate
   cake mix
19.8-oz. pkg. brownie mix

3 eggs, beaten
3/4 c. oil
3/4 c. water

Mix all ingredients together in a large mixing bowl; drop 3 inches apart by tablespoonfuls onto ungreased baking sheets. Bake at 325 degrees for 8 to 10 minutes. Let cool on baking sheets for 2 minutes before removing to wire racks to cool completely.

Nuts just take up space where chocolate ought to be.
-Unknown

Grammy's Chocolate Cookies

Makes 8 dozen

2 c. all-purpose flour
3/4 c. baking cocoa
1 t. baking soda
1/2 t. salt

1-1/4 c. butter, softened
2-1/2 c. sugar, divided
2 eggs, beaten
2 t. vanilla extract

Combine flour, cocoa, baking soda and salt together in a mixing bowl; set aside. Blend butter, 2 cups sugar and eggs until light and fluffy, about 2 minutes; add vanilla. Gradually add dry ingredients to butter mixture; blend well. Cover dough with plastic wrap; chill one hour. Roll dough into one-inch balls; dip tops into remaining sugar. Place on lightly greased baking sheets about 1-1/2 inches apart; bake at 350 degrees for 8 minutes. Cool on baking sheets for 5 minutes before transferring to a wire rack to cool completely.

Pipe melted chocolate into the fork prints on peanut butter
cookies...a winning combination!

Double Chocolate Brownies

Makes one dozen

3 1-oz. sqs. unsweetened
   baking chocolate
6 T. butter
2/3 c. all-purpose flour
1/8 t. salt

1-1/3 c. sugar
3 eggs, beaten
1 t. vanilla extract
3/4 c. semi-sweet chocolate
   chips

Melt together unsweetened chocolate and butter in a small, heavy saucepan over low heat. Stir until smooth; remove from heat and let cool slightly. Stir together flour and salt; set aside. Gradually stir sugar into cooled chocolate mixture. Add eggs and vanilla; stir just to combine. Fold in flour mixture. Spread in an 8"x8" baking pan sprayed with non-stick vegetable spray. Sprinkle with chocolate chips; bake at 325 degrees for 30 to 35 minutes. Use a knife to spread melted chips over the surface. Let cool; cut into squares.

Looking for a sweet & simple snack on the run? Toss together raisins, banana chips, nuts and candy-coated chocolates...so tasty!

Pumpkin-Chocolate Chip Cookies *Makes 3-1/2 dozen*

1/2 c. margarine, softened
1-1/2 c. sugar
1 egg, beaten
1 c. canned pumpkin
1 t. vanilla extract
2-1/2 c. all-purpose flour
1 t. baking powder

1/2 t. salt
1 t. nutmeg
1 t. cinnamon
6-oz. pkg. semi-sweet chocolate
   chips
Optional: chopped nuts

Blend margarine and sugar together until creamy; set aside. Combine egg, pumpkin and vanilla; blend into margarine mixture and set aside. Mix dry ingredients together; blend into pumpkin mixture. Fold in chocolate chips and nuts, if desired. Drop by tablespoonfuls onto lightly greased baking sheets; bake at 350 degrees until golden, about 8 minutes. Let cool on baking sheets for 2 minutes before removing to wire rack to cool completely.

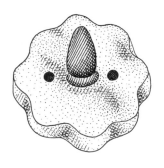

For double-chocolate decadence, dip half (or all!) of each
Chocolate Cut-Out into melted chocolate...irresistible!

Chocolate Cut-Outs

Makes 2 to 3 dozen

1 egg, beaten
2/3 c. butter, softened
3/4 c. sugar
1 t. vanilla extract
1/4 c. baking cocoa

1-1/2 c. all-purpose flour
1 t. baking powder
1/2 t. salt
Optional: frosting, colored sugar

Combine egg, butter and sugar; blend until creamy. Add remaining ingredients except frosting and colored sugar. Form dough into 2 flattened rounds; chill. Roll out on a floured surface to 1/8-inch thickness. Cut with cookie cutters as desired; place on ungreased baking sheets. Bake at 350 degrees for 8 to 10 minutes. Let cool; frost and sprinkle with sugar, if desired.

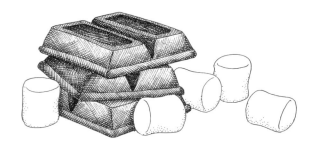

Paper baking cups are available in many sizes and are
a great way to serve individual desserts...especially for
those ooey-gooey treats!

Sweet & Sticky S'more Bars

Makes 1-1/2 dozen

2 c. graham cracker crumbs
1/3 c. sugar
1/4 t. salt

1/2 c. butter, melted
2 c. semi-sweet chocolate chips
4 c. mini marshmallows

Blend together the first 4 ingredients; set aside one cup mixture. Press remaining mixture into an ungreased 13"x9" baking pan and bake at 350 degrees for 10 minutes, or until golden. Let cool. Melt chocolate in a double boiler and spread over cooled crust. Layer on marshmallows, pressing gently into warm chocolate; top with one cup reserved graham cracker mixture. Broil 2 inches from heat source until marshmallows are lightly golden; cool and cut into squares.

The easiest mocha ever...add a tablespoon or 2 of hot cocoa
mix to your morning coffee and stir to dissolve.
Who needs a fancy café?

Chocolate No-Bake Cookies   *Makes 1-1/2 to 2 dozen*

2 c. sugar
3 T. baking cocoa
1/2 c. butter
1/2 c. milk

1/2 c. creamy peanut butter
1/4 t. vanilla extract
3 c. quick-cooking oats,
    uncooked

Mix together sugar and cocoa in a saucepan. Add butter and milk;
stir over medium-high heat until butter melts. Bring to a boil for one
minute; remove from heat. Add peanut butter and vanilla; mix well.
Slowly stir in oats, making sure all oats are covered. Drop by
tablespoonfuls onto wax paper; let harden.

Thank a favorite friend with a basketful of mint chocolate
brownies...tie on a silly little note that says,
"We were 'mint' to be friends!"

Pearls 'n Chocolate Cookies

Makes 2-1/2 dozen

2-1/4 c. all-purpose flour
2/3 c. baking cocoa
1 t. baking soda
1/2 t. salt
1 c. butter, softened

3/4 c. sugar
2/3 c. brown sugar, packed
1 t. vanilla extract
2 eggs, beaten
1-1/2 c. white chocolate chips

Combine flour, cocoa, baking soda and salt in a mixing bowl; set aside. In a large bowl, beat butter, sugar, brown sugar and vanilla until creamy. Stir in eggs, one at a time. Gradually add flour mixture; stir in white chocolate chips. Drop by tablespoonfuls onto ungreased baking sheets; bake for 9 to 10 minutes. Let stand for 2 minutes on baking sheets before removing to wire racks to cool completely.

Dirt for dessert? Here's a fun serving idea! Line the inside of a new clay pot with wax paper and then fill with softened ice cream. Cover ice cream with crushed chocolate cookies and slip a pinwheel into the center. Everyone will love eating their "dirt"!

German Chocolate Cake

Serves 10 to 12

18-1/4 oz. pkg. white cake mix
5.9-oz. pkg. instant chocolate
    pudding mix
1 c. milk
1 c. water
3 eggs, separated
1 c. evaporated milk

1 c. sugar
1/2 c. butter, melted
1 t. vanilla extract
1-1/3 c. sweetened flaked
    coconut
1 c. chopped pecans

Combine cake mix, pudding mix, milk, water and egg whites in a large bowl; beat at medium speed for 2 minutes. Pour into 2 greased and floured round cake pans. Bake at 350 degrees for 25 to 35 minutes. Cool 10 minutes in pans; remove to wire racks to cool completely before frosting. Set aside. Slightly beat egg yolks in a saucepan; add evaporated milk, sugar, butter and vanilla. Cook over medium heat, stirring constantly, for about 12 minutes, until thick. Remove from heat; add coconut and pecans. Beat until mixture is cool and spreadable. Frost cake.

When a chocolate cake recipe calls for the pan to be greased
and floured, use baking cocoa instead of flour. The cocoa will
keep a white ring from forming around the cake.

Midnight Chocolate Cake

Serves 15 to 18

3-1/2 oz. pkg. cook & serve
   chocolate pudding mix
18-1/2 oz. pkg. chocolate cake
   mix

12-oz. pkg. semi-sweet
   chocolate chips

Prepare pudding according to package directions; blend in cake mix. Spread into a lightly greased and floured 13"x9" baking pan; sprinkle with chocolate chips. Bake at 350 degrees for 20 to 25 minutes.

Chocolate whipped cream... just beat 2 tablespoons each of
baking cocoa and powdered sugar into one cup whipping cream!

Time-Saver Chocolate Cake

2 c. all-purpose flour
2 c. sugar
1/2 c. baking cocoa, divided
1 c. margarine, softened and
    divided
1 c. water
1 t. vanilla extract

1/2 c. buttermilk
1/2 t. baking soda
1 t. cinnamon
2 eggs, beaten
6 T. milk
16-oz. pkg. powdered sugar

Combine flour and sugar in a large mixing bowl; set aside. Combine
1/4 cup baking cocoa, 1/2 cup margarine, water and vanilla in a
saucepan; bring to a boil, stirring often. Remove from heat; pour into
flour mixture. Add buttermilk, baking soda, cinnamon and eggs; mix
well. Spread in a greased and floured 13"x9" baking pan; bake at
350 degrees, for 30 minutes, or until a toothpick inserted in the center
removes clean. Remove from oven; set aside. Combine remaining
cocoa, margarine and milk in saucepan; bring to a boil, stirring
constantly. Remove from heat; stir in powdered sugar until smooth
and creamy. Spread over warm cake.

Decorating dessert plates is so easy. Try piping melted chocolate in fun designs and words. You can also use simple kitchen utensils (forks work great) as stencils... just lay them on the plate, sprinkle baking cocoa or powdered sugar over top and remove to show off designs. Clever!

Blue-Ribbon Chocolate Cake

Serves 12 to 16

1/4 c. butter, softened
1/4 c. shortening
2 c. sugar
1 t. vanilla extract
2 eggs, beaten
3/4 c. baking cocoa

1-3/4 c. all-purpose flour
1/4 t. baking powder
3/4 t. salt
1-3/4 c. milk
15-1/2 oz. can chocolate
 frosting

Blend butter, shortening, sugar and vanilla until fluffy; stir in eggs and set aside. Combine cocoa, flour, baking powder and salt; add alternately with milk to sugar mixture. Blend well; pour into 2 greased and floured 9" round baking pans. Bake at 350 degrees for 30 to 35 minutes; let cool and spread with chocolate frosting.

I could give up chocolate, but I'm not a quitter.
-Unknown

Caramel Fudge Cake

18-1/4 oz. pkg. chocolate cake
   mix
1/2 c. margarine
14-oz. pkg. caramels,
   unwrapped

14-oz. can sweetened
   condensed milk
1 c. chopped pecans

Prepare cake according to package directions; pour 2 cups of batter into a greased 13"x9" baking pan. Bake at 350 degrees for 15 minutes; set aside. In a saucepan, melt margarine and caramels; remove from heat. Add condensed milk; stir well and pour over cake. Spread remaining cake batter over caramel mixture. Sprinkle with pecans; bake for an additional 30 minutes. Cool before serving.

Turn a chocolate doughnut into a double-chocolatey treat!
Slice a doughnut in half, fill with softened chocolate ice cream
and then replace the second slice...easy!

Luscious Chocolate Cake

Serves 8 to 10

2 c. all-purpose flour
2 t. baking soda
1/2 t. salt
1/2 c. butter, softened
2 c. sugar
3 eggs
1-1/2 t. vanilla extract

3 1-oz. sqs. unsweetened
    baking chocolate, melted
    and cooled
4-oz. pkg. instant chocolate
    pudding mix
1 c. sour cream
1/2 c. milk

Combine flour, baking soda and salt; set aside. In a large mixing bowl, beat butter and sugar with an electric mixer on medium speed; add eggs and beat until light and fluffy. Beat in vanilla and chocolate; add flour mixture alternately with pudding mix and sour cream. Stir in milk to make a thin batter. Pour into a lightly greased 8" springform pan; bake at 350 degrees for 50 to 55 minutes or until cake tester comes out clean. Cool in pan for 10 minutes; turn out onto wire rack to cool completely.

Say "Welcome" to new co-workers...leave a basket of chocolate candy, cookies or brownies on their desk. If they're new to town, be sure to include directions to all the best places for lunch, the bank and the post office.

Chocolate-Oatmeal Cake

Serves 12 to 16

1 c. quick-cooking oats,
    uncooked
1-1/2 c. boiling water
1/2 c. shortening
1/2 c. sugar
2 eggs, beaten
1 c. all-purpose flour
1/2 c. baking cocoa

1 t. baking soda
1/2 t. salt
1 t. vanilla extract
1/4 c. milk
1/2 c. brown sugar, packed
2 T. butter, softened
1 c. sweetened flaked coconut

Combine oats and boiling water; set aside for 20 minutes. Blend shortening, sugar and eggs in a mixing bowl; stir in oat mixture, flour, cocoa, baking soda, salt and vanilla, beating until smooth. Pour into a greased 13"x9" baking pan; bake at 350 degrees for 30 minutes. Combine remaining ingredients, blending well; spread over warm cake. Return to oven for 3 to 5 minutes, until golden.

An incredible treat...fill flat-bottomed ice cream cones
half-full of chocolatey brownie batter, place on a baking sheet
and bake at 350 degrees for 20 minutes. When cooled,
top with scoops of ice cream!

3-Layer Chocolate Cake

Serves 12

1 c. butter, softened
1-3/4 c. sugar
1 t. vanilla extract
3 eggs
1 c. baking cocoa
1 t. baking soda

1/4 t. salt
2-1/4 c. all-purpose flour
1-1/2 t. baking powder
1-3/4 c. milk
15-1/2 oz. can fudge frosting

Blend butter, sugar and vanilla together in a large mixing bowl until light and fluffy. Add eggs; beat well and set aside. Sift together all dry ingredients and alternately add with milk to sugar mixture. Divide evenly into 3 greased 9" round cake pans; bake at 350 degrees for 25 to 30 minutes. Cool for 10 minutes in pans. When completely cool, spread with fudge frosting.

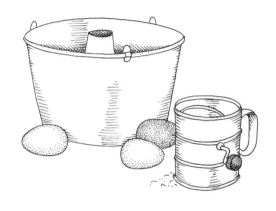

You can add up to 3 tablespoons of baking cocoa
to boxed cake mixes for extra zip!

Hot Cocoa Bundt® Cake

Serves 10 to 12

1/2 c. shortening
3/4 c. sugar
2 eggs, beaten
1-1/2 c. all-purpose flour
3/4 t. salt

2 t. baking powder
2/3 c. milk
2 envs. hot chocolate mix
Optional: powdered sugar

Blend shortening, sugar and eggs until mixture is fluffy. Add flour, salt and baking powder alternately with milk, beating well after each addition. Spoon one-third of the batter into a greased Bundt® pan; sprinkle with one envelope hot chocolate mix. Add another third of batter; sprinkle with remaining hot chocolate mix, then remaining batter. Bake at 350 degrees for 35 minutes, or until a toothpick comes out clean. Let stand 5 minutes in pan; turn out onto wire rack to cool completely. Dust with powdered sugar, if desired.

Yummy invitations! For your next party, try hand-delivering big chocolate cookies piped with the occasion, date and time in vanilla or peanut butter frosting. You're sure to get instant RSVP's!

Simple Chocolate Cake

Serves 8 to 10

3 c. all-purpose flour
3 c. sugar
3 eggs
3/4 c. baking cocoa

1 T. baking powder
1 T. baking soda
3/4 c. oil
3 c. boiling water

Mix first 7 ingredients together; add water and beat for 2 minutes.
Pour batter into a greased 13"x9" baking pan. Bake at 350 degrees
for 40 to 45 minutes, or until a toothpick inserted into the center
removes clean.

Chocolate shavings look so delicate but are really simple
to make. Just pull a vegetable peeler across a bar
of chocolate and watch it curl!

Easy-As-Pie Chocolate Pie

1/2 c. milk
24 marshmallows
4 1.45-oz. chocolate candy bars
    with almonds, chopped

2 c. frozen whipped topping,
    thawed and divided
9-inch pie crust, baked

Heat milk and marshmallows in a double boiler until marshmallows melt; stir in chocolate bars until melted. Remove from heat; cool. Add one cup whipped topping; stir well and pour into pie crust. Spread with remaining whipped topping; refrigerate until firm.

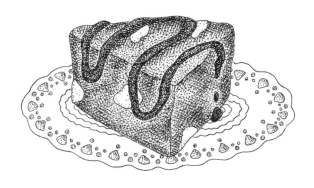

Personalize each dessert. Fill a pastry bag with melted chocolate and drizzle designs on wax paper...try hearts, stars and friends' initials. Freeze chocolate until firm, then use to top each serving of pie, cake or pudding.

Peanut Butter & Fudge Pie

Serves 4 to 6

1/2 c. creamy peanut butter
1/4 c. honey
1 qt. vanilla ice cream, softened
   and divided
6-oz. graham cracker crust

1/2 c. cashews, chopped and
   divided
6-oz. jar fudge ice cream
   topping, divided
Garnish: whipped topping

Combine peanut butter and honey; blend in ice cream. Spoon half into pie crust; sprinkle with half the cashews. Drizzle half the fudge topping over cashews; spoon remaining ice cream mixture over top. Sprinkle with remaining cashews and drizzle with fudge topping. Freeze until firm, about 6 hours. Garnish with whipped topping.

Keep chocolate in a cool, odor-free place. Under ideal conditions, chocolate shelf life is one year for dark chocolate, 10 months for milk chocolate and 8 months for white chocolate.

Chocolate Chip Pie

Serves 8

1/2 c. all-purpose flour
1/2 c. sugar
1/2 c. brown sugar, packed
2 eggs, beaten

3/4 c. butter, softened
1 c. semi-sweet chocolate chips
1 c. chopped walnuts
9-inch pie crust

Blend flour, sugar and brown sugar into eggs; add butter, mixing well. Fold in chocolate chips and walnuts; pour into pie crust. Bake at 325 degrees for 55 minutes to one hour, or until knife inserted into middle of pie comes out clean.

Chocolate is best melted in a double boiler, but you can use
a microwave if you're careful...use short bursts of
10 to 15 seconds of power, checking between bursts.

Cherry Chocolate Pie

2 21-oz. cans cherry pie filling
9-inch pie crust, baked
1/2 c. sliced almonds
3 T. semi-sweet baking
chocolate

1 T. butter
Garnish: whipped topping and
chocolate syrup

Spoon pie filling into cooled pie crust; bake at 350 degrees until bubbly, about 35 minutes. Cool. Sprinkle with almonds; set aside. Melt chocolate and butter in a double boiler, stirring constantly; set aside. Garnish pie with whipped topping; drizzle chocolate mixture over top.

For a new twist, turn a banana cream pie into a banana split pie!
Drizzle slices with chocolate topping, nuts and top with a
maraschino cherry!

German Chocolate Pie

Serves 6

2 1-oz. sqs. German sweet
   baking chocolate
1 c. butter
3 eggs
2 T. all-purpose flour
1 c. sugar

1 t. vanilla extract
1 c. chopped pecans
1/2 c. sweetened flaked coconut
Garnish: whipped cream,
   shaved chocolate and
   pecans

Melt chocolate and butter in a saucepan over low heat; let cool and set aside. Beat eggs, flour, sugar and vanilla together with an electric mixer for 3 minutes on high speed. Pour chocolate mixture over egg mixture and beat for 3 additional minutes. Add pecans and coconut. Pour into a well greased 9" pie plate. Bake at 350 degrees for 25 to 30 minutes. Let cool. Top with whipped cream and garnish with shaved chocolate and pecans. Serve immediately.

A special thanks for all those special deliveries...add a tin of homemade chocolate candy or brownies to your mailbox for the mail carrier!

Hot Fudge Pie

Serves 8

1/2 c. butter, melted
3 T. baking cocoa
1/4 c. all-purpose flour
2 eggs, beaten
1 c. sugar

1 t. vanilla extract
1 c. chopped pecans
9-inch pie crust
Garnish: whipped topping and
    hot fudge sauce

Stir butter and cocoa together; add next 5 ingredients and mix well.
Pour into pie crust; bake at 350 degrees for 30 minutes. Cool; top
with garnishes as desired before serving.

Chocolate first arrived in the American colonies in 1765! Hurrah!

Crunchy Chocolate Pie

Serves 8

3 T. creamy peanut butter
2 T. honey
2 c. crispy rice cereal

1-1/2 oz. pkg. instant chocolate
   pudding mix
2 c. milk

Combine peanut butter and honey in a saucepan over low heat; stir until peanut butter is melted. Remove from heat; stir in cereal to coat. Press into bottom and up sides of a greased 8" pie plate; freeze for one hour. Set aside. Prepare pudding mix with milk according to package directions; spread over cereal crust. Chill for at least one hour before serving.

Junk food? Cocoa beans are a good source of protein,
fiber, B vitamins, iron and phosphorus!

Chocolate Pecan Pie

Serves 8

8 1-oz. sqs. semi-sweet baking
   chocolate, divided
2 T. butter
9-inch pie crust
3 eggs, beaten and divided

1/4 c. brown sugar, packed
1 c. corn syrup
1 t. vanilla extract
1-1/2 c. pecan halves

Coarsely chop 4 squares chocolate; set aside. In a large bowl, microwave remaining chocolate and butter together on high setting for one to 3 minutes, stirring occasionally, until butter is melted. Stir well until chocolate is completely melted. Brush bottom of pie crust with a small amount of beaten egg; set aside. Stir brown sugar, corn syrup, remaining eggs and vanilla into chocolate mixture; blend. Add nuts and chopped chocolate. Pour into pie crust and bake at 350 degrees for 55 minutes, or until a knife inserted 2 inches from edge of crust comes out clean. Cool on wire rack.

The Easter Bunny is the most popular design
of molded chocolate.

Chocolate Quesadillas

6 8-inch flour tortillas
2 T. butter, melted

1 c. milk chocolate chips
Garnish: vanilla ice cream

Brush both sides of each tortilla with melted butter; arrange in a single layer on an ungreased baking sheet. Sprinkle chocolate chips on half of each tortilla; fold over tortillas. Bake for 4 to 6 minutes at 450 degrees until golden. Top each with a scoop of vanilla ice cream.

Chocolate dessert cups are easy to make. Just paint paper muffin cups with melted chocolate, chill until firm and peel off the paper. Serve on a chilled plate so the cups will keep their shape.

Chocolate Mousse

Serves 4 to 6

6-oz. pkg. semi-sweet chocolate
    chips
1/2 c. butter
3 pasteurized eggs, separated

2 T. sugar
3/4 c. whipping cream
1/2 t. vanilla extract

In a double boiler, melt chocolate and butter over low heat; pour into a bowl and let cool to room temperature. Add egg yolks to chocolate and stir well; set aside. In a separate mixing bowl, beat egg whites to soft peaks, adding sugar gradually. Whisk a small amount of egg white into chocolate mixture, then gently fold in the rest. Whip cream and vanilla together until stiff; fold into chocolate mixture. Spoon into serving dishes and chill before serving.

Hot chocolate is a great bedtime beverage...although the caffeine in it is a stimulant, the hot milk acts as a sleep inducer.

Chocolate Lover's Bread Pudding

Serves 6 to 8

4 white bread slices, crusts
    removed
4 c. milk
1-oz. sq. unsweetened baking
    chocolate, chopped

2 eggs, beaten
1 c. sugar
1 t. vanilla extract

Tear bread into bite-size pieces and place in a small saucepan. Stir in milk and chocolate; bring to a boil, stirring constantly. Remove from heat. Blend eggs and sugar together; gradually pour mixture over eggs, stirring constantly. Stir in vanilla and pour into a 2-quart casserole dish. Place dish in a larger pan filled with water one to 2 inches deep; bake at 350 degrees for one hour, or until a knife inserted into the center comes out clean.

Make a treasure chest for your little pirates filled with
candy necklaces, "jewel" candy rings and golden-wrapped
chocolate coins...draw up a map and boys & girls alike
will love searching for the booty!

Chocolate Dumplings

1-oz. sq. unsweetened baking
   chocolate
1 c. water
1/4 t. salt, divided
2 T. butter, divided
1 c. plus 2 T. sugar, divided

1/2 t. cornstarch
1/2 c. all-purpose flour
1/2 t. baking powder
1 egg
1/4 t. vanilla extract
2 T. milk

In a saucepan over medium heat, combine chocolate, water,
1/8 teaspoon salt and one tablespoon butter; set aside. Combine one
cup sugar with cornstarch; stir into chocolate mixture. Return to
medium heat for 2 minutes; reduce heat to low and simmer, stirring
often, while making dumplings. In a large mixing bowl, mix flour,
baking powder, remaining salt, sugar and butter together; set aside.
Blend egg, vanilla and milk in another bowl; add to flour mixture.
Bring chocolate mixture to a slight boil; drop in tablespoonfuls of
batter. Cover pan tightly; simmer for 20 minutes. Do not open lid.

For an easy sweet & salty treat, pop your favorite microwave popcorn, spread out on a wax paper-lined baking sheet, and drizzle with melted chocolate chips. Let harden, then store in airtight containers. Delicious!

Steamed Chocolate Pudding

Serves 4 to 6

1 egg
1 c. sugar
1/3 c. plus 2 T. butter, softened
2 1-oz. sqs. unsweetened
    baking chocolate, melted
1-3/4 c. all-purpose flour
1/2 t. salt

1/4 t. cream of tartar
1/4 t. baking soda
1 c. milk
1 c. powdered sugar
1 T. half-and-half
1 t. vanilla extract

Beat egg, sugar, 2 tablespoons butter and chocolate together, mixing well. Combine flour, salt, cream of tartar and baking soda; stir into egg mixture. Slowly add milk. Pour into a greased one-quart mold; place mold in a larger pan filled with water 3 to 4 inches deep. Steam over medium-high heat for 3 hours, adding more water if necessary as it evaporates; set aside. Blend remaining butter, powdered sugar, half-and-half and vanilla; beat until fluffy. Chill until cold, but not hard. Serve with pudding.

Dress up your ice cream...dip waffle cones into melted chocolate and sprinkle with jimmies. Set each in a glass to let chocolate harden, then fill with scoops of ice cream.

Chocolate Rapture

Serves 6 to 8

21-1/2 oz. pkg. brownie mix
Optional: 1/4 c. coffee liqueur
2 2-oz. pkgs. chocolate mousse
    mix
12-oz. container frozen whipped
    topping, thawed

8 1.4-oz. chocolate-covered
    toffee candy bars, finely
    chopped
1 c. chopped pecans

Prepare and bake brownies according to package directions; let cool.
Poke holes in brownies with a fork and brush with liqueur, if using.
Coarsely crumble brownies and place half in a large glass serving bowl;
set aside. Prepare mousse according to package directions, except do
not chill after beating. Spread half the mousse over brownies in bowl;
top with half the whipped topping. Sprinkle with half the toffee and
half the nuts. Repeat layers; cover and chill several hours or overnight
before serving.

Make dessert extra fun for the kids. Bake a chocolate-covered mint patty inside one cupcake...whoever gets that one wins a prize!

Black Forest Cupcakes

Makes one dozen

1 c. all-purpose flour
1/2 t. baking powder
1/2 t. baking soda
1/2 t. salt
6 T. butter, softened
1 c. sugar
2 eggs

2 1-oz. sqs. unsweetened
   baking chocolate, melted
   and cooled
1 t. vanilla extract
1/2 c. milk
16-oz. can chocolate frosting
12-oz. can cherry pastry filling

Whisk flour, baking powder, baking soda and salt together; set aside.
Beat butter with an electric mixer on high speed until fluffy; gradually
blend in sugar. Continue blending to keep mixture light and fluffy;
beat in eggs, one at a time. Add melted chocolate and vanilla;
alternately blend in flour mixture and milk until just mixed. Spoon
into 12 paper-lined muffin cups, filling two-thirds full; bake at
350 degrees for 15 to 20 minutes. Cool 15 minutes on a wire rack
before removing; spread with frosting and top each with a
tablespoonful of cherry pastry filling.

Dip the rim of a dessert glass in melted chocolate and immediately coat the chocolate with chopped nuts. Refrigerate until firm, then when it's time to serve dessert, add a big scoop of Chocolate Frostie Ice Cream!

Chocolate Frostie Ice Cream

Serves 16 to 20

1/2 gal. chocolate whole milk
12-oz. container frozen whipped
    topping, thawed

14-oz. can sweetened
    condensed milk

Combine all ingredients; mix well. Pour into an electric ice cream
maker; freeze according to manufacturer's instructions.

Old-fashioned gelatin molds, tart tins and vintage drinking glasses
are just right for filling with bite-size chocolates...place several
around the room for easy snacking.

Chocolate-Covered Cherries *Makes about 4-1/2 dozen*

16-oz. pkg. powdered sugar
1 c. margarine, softened
2 t. vanilla extract
1 T. evaporated milk
2 10-oz. jars maraschino
    cherries, drained

8 1-oz. sqs. semi-sweet baking
    chocolate
1/4 sq. paraffin

Combine sugar, margarine, vanilla and evaporated milk in a mixing bowl; mix well. Dip each cherry in sugar mixture to coat; chill overnight. Melt chocolate and paraffin in a saucepan over medium-low heat, stirring to combine; dip cherries in chocolate mixture and place on wax paper to dry.

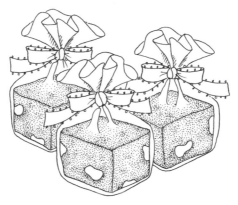

Enjoy s'mores without a campfire! Spread marshmallow creme on whole graham crackers and then spread with softened rocky road ice cream. Top with another graham cracker, press firmly and freeze until solid.

Creamy Fudge

Makes 6-1/2 pounds

1 lb. butter, softened
1 lb. pasteurized processed
   cheese spread, cubed
4 16-oz. pkgs. powdered sugar

1 c. baking cocoa
1 t. vanilla extract
2 c. chopped nuts

In a saucepan, heat butter and cheese over medium-low heat until melted; set aside. Sift together powdered sugar and cocoa in a large bowl. Add butter mixture; mix well. Stir in vanilla and nuts. Divide evenly between 3 greased 8"x8" baking pans; spread evenly, cool and cut into small squares.

Remember the tall candy jars at the corner store? Pick one
up at a flea market and fill it with chocolate-covered,
sprinkle-dipped pretzel rods for a colorful, extra-sweet gift.

Chocolate Pretzels

Makes about 3 dozen

3/4 c. butter, softened
3/4 c. sugar
1 egg
1 t. vanilla extract
2 c. all-purpose flour

1/3 c. baking cocoa
2 t. baking powder
1 t. salt
Garnish: assorted sprinkles

Blend butter and sugar with an electric mixer on medium speed until light and fluffy; blend in egg and vanilla. Add flour, cocoa, baking powder and salt until just combined; divide dough in half. Wrap one half in plastic wrap; set aside. Shape remaining dough by tablespoonfuls into 9-inch long ropes. Twist into pretzel shapes; lightly press into sprinkles. Arrange sprinkle-side up on lightly greased baking sheets; repeat with remaining dough. Bake at 350 degrees for 15 minutes; remove to a wire rack to cool completely.

At your next camp-out, slice an unpeeled banana half-way through lengthwise. Spoon in one or 2 teaspoons each of semi-sweet chocolate chips and mini marshmallows, then sprinkle with a little brown sugar. Wrap it all up in aluminum foil, sealing the ends. Place it on the campfire coals, seam-side up and let it cook for about 7 minutes. Yum!

Chocolate-Raspberry Fudge

Makes 3 dozen

14-oz. can sweetened
   condensed milk
3 c. semi-sweet chocolate chips
1-1/2 t. vanilla extract

1/4 t. salt
1/4 c. whipping cream
3/4 t. raspberry extract
6-oz. pkg. raspberry chips

Line an 8"x8" baking pan with aluminum foil; cover with a layer of wax paper. Set aside. Heat condensed milk in a double boiler over medium heat for 3 to 4 minutes; gradually add chocolate chips. Stir constantly until melted and smooth; add vanilla and salt. Spread into prepared pan; cool to room temperature and set aside. Heat cream in a heavy saucepan until just boiling; add raspberry extract, stirring to mix. Add raspberry chips; reduce heat to medium-low. Stir until chips are melted and mixture is smooth; cool to room temperature and pour over fudge. Refrigerate overnight. Cut into small squares to serve.

For clever placecards, write names on the handles of
chocolate-dipped wooden spoons with permanent markers.
Guests can find their seats, flavor their coffees
or cocoas, and won't pick up the wrong mug!

Chocolate-Topped Toffee

Makes about 2 cups

1/2 c. butter
1/2 t. salt
1 c. sugar
1/4 c. water

12-oz. pkg. semi-sweet
  chocolate chips
1 c. chopped pecans or almonds,
  divided

Combine butter, salt, sugar and water in a 2-quart saucepan. Cook over medium heat, stirring constantly, until mixture boils. Cook without stirring until mixture reaches soft crack stage, or 270 to 289 degrees on a candy thermometer. Pour onto a greased baking sheet and cool until set. Melt chocolate chips and spread half over toffee. Sprinkle with half the chopped nuts. Chill until set, then loosen toffee with knife and flip over. Spread with remaining chocolate and sprinkle with remaining nuts. Chill until set. Break into bite-size pieces and store in an airtight container.

Arrange mini pretzels on a wax paper-lined microwave-safe plate. Top each with 5 or 6 semi-sweet chocolate chips and microwave on high for 15 to 30 seconds until chocolate melts. Press mini candy-coated chocolates into the warm chocolate and let cool. So simple!

Chocolate-Peanut Candy *Makes about 8 dozen*

1 T. oil
3 T. baking cocoa
24-oz. pkg. white melting
  chocolate
12-oz. pkg. semi-sweet
  chocolate chips

2 c. unsalted dry-roasted
  peanuts
2 c. salted dry-roasted peanuts

Place oil, cocoa, white chocolate and chocolate chips in a 5-quart slow cooker. Cover and cook on high setting until chocolate is melted and smooth, about 15 to 20 minutes; turn off heat and add peanuts. Stir well. Drop by teaspoonfuls onto wax paper; let cool.

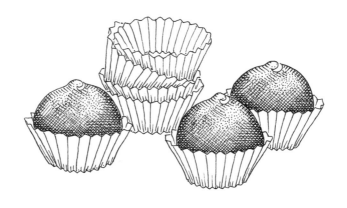

Make a truffle tree! Poke a toothpick halfway into a foil-wrapped truffle and the remaining half into a foam tree form. Continue until form is filled...what a delicious centerpiece!

Chocolate-Raspberry Truffles *Makes 1-1/2 to 2 dozen*

1/2 c. semi-sweet chocolate
    chips
1/2 c. raspberry chips

5-1/2 T. butter
3 T. whipping cream
Garnish: powdered sugar

Combine first 4 ingredients in a microwave-safe bowl. Melt 1-1/2 to
2 minutes; stir until creamy and combined. Mixture will be thin. Freeze
exactly one hour. Shape into walnut-size balls; roll in powdered sugar.
Store in refrigerator until ready to serve.

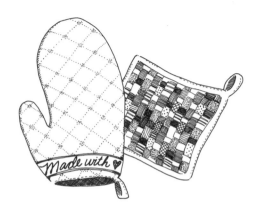

Teachers, bus drivers and babysitters will love a hot cocoa
jar mix. Simply pour some hot cocoa mix into a jar, top with
a layer of mini marshmallows and a layer of chocolate chips,
seal tightly and top with a pretty jar topper. Be creative...try
with chocolate-mint or chocolate-cherry candies too!

Chocolate-Covered Espresso Beans

Makes about 2 cups

1 c. espresso beans

1 to 1-1/2 c. bittersweet
chocolate chips, melted

Spread espresso beans about 1/2 inch apart in a wax paper-lined jelly-roll pan; spoon half the chocolate over beans. Chill in refrigerator until hard; turn beans over and top with remaining chocolate. Repeat chilling. Store in an airtight container.

No chocolate treat is complete without ice-cold milk! Serve it up in old-fashioned milk bottles from the flea market...kids will love it!

Chocolate-Covered Raisin Fudge *Makes 1-1/2 dozen*

1-1/2 c. sugar
2/3 c. evaporated milk
2 T. butter
1/4 t. salt
2 c. mini marshmallows
1-1/2 c. semi-sweet chocolate
  chips

2 c. chocolate-covered raisins,
  divided
1 t. vanilla extract
1/2 c. chopped nuts

Combine sugar, evaporated milk, butter and salt in a heavy saucepan; bring to a rolling boil over medium heat, stirring constantly. Boil for 4 to 5 minutes; remove from heat. Stir in marshmallows, chocolate chips, one cup raisins, vanilla and nuts. Stir continuously for one minute until marshmallows are melted. Pour into an 8"x8" baking pan lined with aluminum foil; cool for one minute. Sprinkle remaining raisins on top, pressing in slightly. Chill for 2 hours until firm. Lift from pan and remove foil. Cut into squares.

Make caramel apples double the fun...once the caramel is set,
dip 'em in melted chocolate and chopped nuts!

Chocolatey Bon-Bons

Makes 3-1/2 dozen

2 c. graham cracker crumbs
4 c. powdered sugar
1 c. sweetened flaked coconut
1 c. butter, softened
1 t. vanilla extract

1 c. chunky peanut butter
2 T. shortening
12-oz. pkg. semi-sweet
   chocolate chips

Mix graham cracker crumbs, powdered sugar and coconut together; add butter, vanilla and peanut butter, mixing until combined. Roll mixture into one-inch balls. Melt shortening in a saucepan over low heat; add chocolate chips and stir until chips are melted and mixture is smooth. Dip balls in chocolate mixture and set on wax paper until hardened.

Keep a look-out for old-fashioned teacups at tag sales. They're perfect for filling with warm chocolate pudding, chocolate candies or sipping your favorite mocha coffee.

Chocolate-Peanut Butter Fudge *Makes about 6 dozen*

4 c. powdered sugar
1/4 t. salt
1/4 c. baking cocoa
1 t. vanilla extract

1-1/4 c. creamy or chunky
    peanut butter
1-1/4 c. butter, melted

In a large mixing bowl, mix together powdered sugar, salt, cocoa and vanilla. Stir in peanut butter. Pour butter over top; mix well. Line a 13"x9" baking pan with plastic wrap; press fudge mixture evenly into pan. Refrigerate and cut into squares.

INDEX

INDEX

How Did Gooseberry Patch Get Started?

Gooseberry Patch started in 1984 one day over the backyard fence in Delaware, Ohio. We were next-door neighbors who shared a love of collecting antiques, gardening and country decorating. Though neither of us had any experience (Jo Ann was a first-grade school teacher and Vickie, a flight attendant & legal secretary), we decided to try our hands at the mail-order business. Since we both had young children, this was perfect for us. We could work from our kitchen tables and keep an eye on the kids too! As our children grew, so did our "little" business. We moved into our own building in the country and filled the shelves to the brim with kitchenware, candles, gourmet goodies, enamelware, bowls and our very own line of cookbooks, calendars and organizers! We're so glad you're a part of our **Gooseberry Patch** family!

For a free copy of our **Gooseberry Patch**
catalog, write us, call us or visit us online at:

Gooseberry Patch
600 London Rd.
★ P.O. Box 190 ★
Delaware, OH 43015

1·800·854·6673
www.gooseberrypatch.com